Trusting
the Shepherd

Trusting the Shepherd
the Shepherd
INSIGHTS from PSALM 23

HADDON W. ROBINSON

DISCOVERY HOUSE
P U B L I S H E R S®

Trusting the Shepherd
© 1968, 2002 by Haddon W. Robinson
Revised edition published 2002. Published
in a previous edition as *Psalm 23* by
The Moody Bible Institute of Chicago.

Discovery House Publishers is affiliated with RBC
Ministries, Grand Rapids, Michigan.

Discovery House books are distributed to the trade exclusively
by Barbour Publishing, Inc., Uhrichsville, Ohio.

Unless otherwise stated, all Scripture quotations
are from the Holy Bible: King James Version (KJV). Other
versions used: New King James Version (NKJV), New
International Version (NIV), New American Standard
Bible (NASB).

Book Design: Sherri L. Hoffman

Library of Congress Cataloging-in-Publication Data
Robinson, Haddon W.
  Trusting the shepherd : insights from Psalm 23 /
  Haddon W. Robinson.
    p. cm.
  ISBN 1-57293-070-5
  1. Bible. O. T. Psalm XXIII—Meditations. I. Title.
BS1450 23rd+ .R62 2002
223'.206—dc21

2002001592

Printed in the United States of America
10 11 12 13 / CHG / 9 8 7 6

Contents

Introduction: Meet the Shepherd   7

1. Listen and Follow   15
2. Defenseless, Dependent,
   and Helpless   23
3. Time Out   31
4. Rest and Refreshment   39
5. Close to His Heart   49
6. Following the Shepherd   57
7. Deep Darkness   65
8. The Darkest Valley   73
9. His Powerful Love   81
10. Protecting the Sheep   89
11. The Abundance of Faith   97
12. Hope for the Future   105
13. In His Presence   113

Introduction Meet the Shepherd

"The LORD is my shepherd."

*T*he Twenty-third Psalm stands as the classic song of the Psalter. Though of ancient origin, like all great classics it does not wear out. As John Keats assured us:

A thing of beauty is a joy forever:
Its loveliness increases; it will never
Pass into nothingness . . . .

Literary critics value the Twenty-third Psalm as a masterpiece of lyric poetry. But this exquisite little psalm has not won its place in our hearts because of the praise of scholars. It is ordinary people everywhere who have received it gladly and turned to it constantly through the centuries. At first thought, that might surprise us, for the majority of men and women do not read poetry. Or if they do, it's often the kind found on greeting cards—simple, easily understood sentiments about life.

But the Twenty-third Psalm is not a simple little poem, nor is it easy to understand. Its imagery conceals as well as reveals, and not every commentator interprets it in the same way. For some, the entire psalm is about sheep and their shepherd. But others insist that only the first three verses talk about sheep. The last three verses, they feel, describe a dinner guest with his host. Still others insist that three pictures can be found in the psalm: a shepherd with his sheep (verses 1 and 2), a guide and a traveler (verses 3 and 4), and a host entertaining his guest (verses 5 and 6). If scholars disagree, we might suppose that ordinary folks would throw up their hands in confusion. Yet they do not.

Understanding the Twenty-third Psalm can also be difficult because its imagery is foreign to city dwellers. In saying, "The LORD is my shepherd; I shall not want," the psalmist compares God to a weather-driven shepherd. To appreciate this metaphor, we have to leave our air-conditioned houses and live for a while under the blazing hot Middle Eastern sun. It might be clearer if we paraphrased the psalm, "The Lord is my mechanic and keeps me in repair." That, of course, would ruin it. To an Israelite shepherd, sheep were not machines.

We value the Twenty-third Psalm because it is personal. God demonstrates the same patient, tireless care of His people that a good shepherd shows for his flock.

Leon Bloy, the French poet and mystic, once described his writings by saying, "I am simply a poor man who seeks his God, sobbing and calling Him along all roads." His was a personal search, but this psalm goes far beyond that. The Twenty-third Psalm affirms a profound personal faith in God; David's faith was that kind. It demonstrates theology at work in the life of someone like me, someone like you.

And it reveals a personal God who relates to us as individuals.

The heading in our Bibles tells us that we're reading "A Psalm of David." David was the greatest king Israel ever had. Yet he was a man filled with the same kind of conflicting passions and bewildering problems that confront any of us. Not only was he the heroic slayer of the giant Goliath, the devoted friend of Jonathan, a lover of music, and an able ruler; he was also a haggard fugitive, an adulterer, and a murderer. David slew his enemies as any ancient monarch did. However, when his predecessor Saul turned against him and became an unrelenting enemy, David refused to kill him, even though he had several opportunities. He took Saul's shield when he could have taken his life. As a father, David had watched his newborn baby die and had sobbed when Absalom, a favorite son, was slain in a rebellion he led against his father. David, therefore, has not left us with mere "beautiful thoughts"; he offers an honest testimony about God, one derived through living life to the hilt.

As a result, though this little psalm was written in a far different time and place than our own, its lessons are as up-to-date as the twenty-first century. As the Quakers put it, it "speaks to our condition." "The meaning and helpfulness of this perfect little psalm can never be exhausted," W. T. Davison observed, "so long as men like sheep wander and need guidance, and so long as they learn to find it in God their shepherd."

Admittedly, we live in complex times; but the Shepherd of whom David wrote has not changed. To our loss, we may have become too sophisticated to trust Him. Faith seems too simple for twenty-first-century living.

A woman admitted to her pastor, " I don't know what it means to trust." He responded, "Tell me, did you ever learn to float?" "Well, I've tried to," she answered. The pastor drove home his point: "Isn't that exactly the reason that you didn't succeed? If you want to float, you must let the water bear you up. The water will do its part if you'll let it." Trusting the Shepherd may seem easy, but anyone who tries it finds that life makes it hard to do.

As one sheep to another, however, I commend the Shepherd of this well-loved psalm to you for your trust.

chapter one Listen and Follow

"The LORD is my shepherd"

*S*omeone has observed that every major portion of Scripture was written by someone having a hard time to men and women having a hard time or about to have a hard time. Although that may not be completely accurate, it is true that the passages of Scripture we love best are the ones to which we turn in times of difficulty. No passage in the Bible, therefore, is more loved or more familiar than this Twenty-third Psalm.

The words of this psalm were probably not penned during the morning of David's life, nor were they written in the noontime of his career. The psalm must have been written during David's twilight years, for they are the words of a man who has lived much and done much;

someone who has greatly sinned and been greatly forgiven.

David writes as a king ruling in the capital city of Jerusalem. As he sits at his desk, memory comes and takes him by the hand and leads him back to his yesterdays. The great arches of his palace disappear, and in their place he sees the azure blue of a Mediterranean sky. David remembers how he cared for the sheep on his father's farm. He reflects on how he led the flocks to green grass and protected the sheep from danger. Then David begins to write, "The LORD is *my* shepherd; I shall not want" (italics added).

Christians sometimes misinterpret this little psalm. They read the opening verse as though it says, "The Lord is my Savior and I'm glad that He is." As wonderful as it is to know that the Christ is your Savior, that is not what this psalm is about. Psalm 23 is one of three psalms that are arranged together in the Psalter: Psalm 22, Psalm 23, and Psalm 24. Each psalm portrays a different work of the Christ for His people. Psalm 22 sketches a prophetic picture of the death of the Savior on the cross. In it, David looks down across the hills of future centuries and sees the hill of Calvary with the suffering Messiah hanging on a tree. Psalm 22, therefore, deals with the "good shepherd [who] lays down his life for the sheep" that we read about in John 10:11 (NIV). Psalm 23, however, deals with the "great shepherd," resurrected for the sheep, described in Hebrews 13:20. Psalm 24 tells of the chief Shepherd who will return to reward those who care for the sheep, as promised in 1 Peter 5:4. Christians who have put their trust in the Christ as the Savior presented in Psalm 22 and who may even look forward to His return as the Sovereign in Psalm 24 may not experience in reality the work of the Shepherd described in Psalm 23. But when David sang of the Christ as Shepherd, he was praising the living God who was present in his daily life and supplied his deepest needs.

The word that David used for "LORD" was the name *Yahweh*. The Hebrew people were so much in awe of that name—and of the God it represented—that they substituted some lesser name for God when they came to it in the public reading of the Scriptures. Yahweh is the God who causes all things to be, and He is the God who brought the nation of Israel into existence. Yet this God who inhabits eternity is the One David speaks of as "my shepherd." He is the God whom Christians trust as well. The Christ in whom we trust as a personal Savior is the same God by whom and through whom and for whom all things were created. That God is great enough to control the universe and guide the destiny of nations, and yet will take care of the needs of your life and mine. Yahweh the Creator visited this little planet of ours and was nailed on a Roman execution rack and died for our sin. It is this great God whose return we eagerly await, and it is Yahweh revealed in Jesus whom we trust with life itself, both for time and for eternity.

That is why a small word in the first verse of Psalm 23 takes on great importance. It is the little word *my*. Millions of religious people know that the Lord is *a* shepherd, but they really don't know that He is *their* Shepherd. How can you know that the God of the universe is actually *your* shepherd? Well, in John 10:27 Jesus declares: "My sheep hear my voice, and I know them, and they follow me: and I give unto them eternal life; and they shall never perish, neither shall any man pluck them out of my hand."

Two simple tests can reveal whether you are one of His flock: "My sheep hear my voice," He said. That is the first test. Do you really listen to what He has to say to you through His Word? Then, Jesus said, "They follow me." That is the second test. Members of Christ's flock follow the leadership He gives them through His Word. It's as simple—and as sublime—as that. Those who belong to the Shepherd from heaven hear His Word and they follow Him.

Who is your shepherd? Your husband or wife? Your pastor? Your parents? Your psychologist? A close friend? As important as these people may be, they never can take the place of the Good Shepherd in your life. They are sheep too. Like you, they need Someone else, just as David did. And you can have Someone else if you give attention to what He says to you in His Word and simply follow His lead in life.

When you come to the place where every detail of your life is placed in Christ's care, you can say with a deep abiding certainty, "The Lord is *my* Shepherd. I shall not want."

chapter two **Defenseless, Dependent, and Helpless**

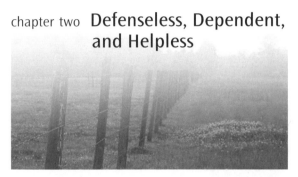

"I shall not want"

When our children were growing up, I played a game with them. I would ask them, "If you could be any animal in the world, what animal would you choose to be?" My daughter usually wanted to be a soft, purring kitten or a mink so that she would have a built-in fur coat. My son wanted to be a lion or a tiger so his friends in the neighborhood would respect him. At other times he wanted to be an elephant so he could squirt water through his nose. Yet, in all the times we played our game, I do not remember either of our children ever choosing to be a sheep.

My children aren't very different from the nations of the world, are they? Many nations have chosen animals to represent them. The United States has taken the soaring eagle as its national symbol. Canada has selected the industrious beaver. Great Britain chose the lion; Russia is represented by the bear. As far as I know, though, no nation has ever adopted a sheep as its emblem.

A sheep represents all the things we do not want to be. Sheep are defenseless, dependent, helpless, and stupid. So when David wrote, "The LORD is my shepherd; I shall not want," by implication he was saying something about himself. He was a sheep. He was defenseless, dependent, and helpless. We might as well admit it: before God we, too, are sheep. As shrewd and courageous as we may think we are, when it comes to the great issues of life, we cannot go it alone. We are defenseless, dependent, helpless, and, to be honest, at times pretty stupid.

We cannot appreciate the Twenty-third Psalm unless we understand that David wrote from the viewpoint of a sheep. And you will never experience the benefits of the psalm unless you are willing to admit that you, too, are a sheep. Because David recognized the Lord as his shepherd, he testifies that he did not want. The phrase "I shall not want" should probably be translated "I shall never be deficient." In other words, "Because the Lord is my shepherd, I shall never want at any time for anything I really need." That opening sentence unlocks the entire psalm.

David is writing about his relationship to a Person. Sometimes we can get so taken up with the particulars of the psalm that we actually ignore the Shepherd. We are attracted to the prospect of green pastures and quiet waters. We resonate to the promise of an overflowing cup.

We grow uneasy at the threat of the journey through the shadow of death. We are attracted to all that the Shepherd does, but we may not recognize that the psalm describes who the Shepherd is. He is at the beginning and the end of the psalm, and all of the experiences described therein are yours only if you

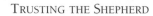

belong to Him. The psalm resembles a string of pearls. Pearls do not look like much unless they are held together by a string. It is God the Shepherd who holds together the benefits of the psalm.

David tells us that if the Lord is your Shepherd, every area and activity of your life is under His direction, protection, and control. Should a Christian complain? Complaining has become a talent in modern life; we shrug it off by saying that it's a safety valve that lets off the pressure of pent-up resentment and frustration. But is that the mark of one of Christ's flock? When we complain, we are really saying that we do not have what we want, we do not like our situation, and the whole arrangement is not quite fair. Yet the psalmist, who knew his share of frustration, wrote, "The LORD is my shepherd; I shall not want." We may quote the first half of this sentence, but often when it comes to trusting our Shepherd and His sufficiency in all our "wants" and "needs," we fail miserably.

We may act patient and kind, but inside we are fuming with anger and discontent.

David, though, believed that the Lord really was his Shepherd. He believed that the Lord planned his life down to the very details of his day, much as a good shepherd does for his flock. When we believe that what we don't like may be part of what He has planned for us today, we can begin to accept His will with joy, knowing that He would not lead us into a difficult circumstance merely to hurt us or desert us. Our Shepherd has our best interests at heart. With that assurance, we can accept any personal slights, unpleasant tasks, or frustrations and still be at peace.

When the Israelites, early in their history as a people, complained about having to live in the wilderness of Sinai, they were punished. Their complaining, says the writer of Hebrews, was a symptom of their unbelief—a lack of trust in their God. I wonder what our complaining is a symptom of.

Why not admit that you are like a sheep, in need of the Shepherd's guidance and care. Then entrust your life to Him; place your well-being in His hands. Accept His direction and selection of events. Let each difficulty become an opportunity to see Him at work in your life. He has said, "'Never will I leave you, never will I forsake you.' So we may say with confidence, 'The Lord is my helper; I will not be afraid. What can man do to me?'" (Hebrews 13:5–6 NIV). If you are one of His flock, you can join David in singing: The Lord is my Shepherd. I am never in want.

chapter three **Time Out**

*"He makes me lie down
in green pastures"*

*T*hree thousand years have passed since David wrote the words of the Twenty-third Psalm. Thirty centuries. That's a long time. The palace in which these words were penned, the harp on which the melody was played, the Book of the Law on which David meditated day and night—all are now buried under the debris of the centuries. Yet the Twenty-third Psalm remains as fresh today as it was in the hour it was first composed.

The psalm has an enduring relevance. These words are among the first that many of us learned as children, and they are often among the last that we whisper in the final dark hours of life, as we look forward to the daybreak of heaven. We speak these words to the dying and repeat them to the grieving who are left behind. The sufferer in the hospital room, the soldier at his lonely post, the immigrant in a strange land, the man and woman burdened down with iron cares—all have found in this psalm strength for their weakness and a lullaby for their fears.

The opening verse strikes the theme of the psalm: If the Lord is your Shepherd, you shall not want. A little girl once quoted this verse, "The Lord is my Shepherd; He's all I want." Although she said it wrong, she was quite right. If the Lord is really your Shepherd, you will not want for rest. David goes on to spell that out when he tells us that the Lord makes His sheep to "lie down in green pastures."

We live in a hectic, hurried, harassed age; an age in which we find it almost impossible to rest. We would like to stop the maddening pace, to stop racing around in circles and wearing ourselves out. We would like to rest. But somehow we fear that if we do take time

out, we will have such a hard time catching up again that it is hardly worth the trouble.

Sheep are rather stupid animals. Like people, they often do not know when or how to rest. Sometimes a flock needs to rest in preparation for a difficult journey before them. But then something will frighten them—perhaps the growl of a mountain lion or the bark of a dog or merely the shout of a child. And instead of resting, the unsettled sheep begin running back and forth across the pasture, wearing themselves out.

The shepherd knows that the sheep need to rest, so he takes them into a pasture filled with green grass. He knows that hungry sheep will not lie down. But even sheep that have eaten their fill can feel agitated and restless. So the shepherd moves in among the flock and, one by one, forces them to lie down in the green pasture. He makes them rest.

Sometimes our Shepherd steps into our situation and forces us to rest. Your "green pasture" may actually be a white-sheeted hospital bed. Many folks who live at a maddening pace have said they could not rest until the Shepherd taught them to do so. But God gives us much more than physical rest. He provides rest for our spirits. The book of Hebrews tells us that one of the things God wants to do for His own is to give us rest. When you come to trust Christ completely, then you will act on God's promises and respond to His command. Life is simplified when you have only one Person to please and only one Master to serve. Living by faith in the Shepherd gives rest to your spirit.

It is quite possible for us, because of unbelief, to be in the midst of green pastures and not recognize them. We see the circumstances into which our Shepherd has led us, but we fail to see them from His vantage point. When our eyes are on the dirt, we fail to see the green grass growing there for our benefit.

When the church was young, Peter, one of the apostles, was persecuted by King Herod

and thrown into prison. Yet even knowing that he might face death by way of an executioner's sword, Peter slept. Apparently, Peter knew that even a prison cell can be a green pasture, when your Shepherd has led you there.

Peter knew the Lord's goodness, and he also trusted in that goodness. There's a great difference between knowledge and appropriation, and the Lord wants to be appropriated. He wants us to know Him *and* trust Him.

It makes all the difference not only to your eternal destiny but also to your rest of spirit whether you say, "Jesus is a Savior" or "Jesus has saved me." And it makes the difference between life and life abundant whether you can say, "The Lord is a Shepherd" or "The Lord is my Shepherd." The Lord Jesus wants to be appropriated. He will never be satisfied, and neither will you, until from the center of your life and the reality of your experience you can say, "He is mine." When that is your honest testimony, you will know His rest. You

will discover, as David did, that Jesus leads His sheep to lie down in green pastures.

chapter four **Rest and Refreshment**

"He leads me beside quiet waters"

*M*y parents came from Scotland and Ireland where it was traditional for congregations to sing the psalms. All of the psalms of the Psalter had been translated into poetry and set to music. Singing the psalms wove their truths into my parents' lives. Often my mother sang a psalm as she worked. Most often it was this version of the Twenty-third Psalm:

> *The Lord's my Shepherd—I'll not want;*
> *He makes me down to lie*
> *In pastures green—He leadeth me*
> *The quiet waters by.*
>
> *My soul He doth restore again,*
> *And me to walk doth make*

Within the paths of righteousness,
E'en for His own name's sake.

Yea, though I walk through death's dark vale,
Yet will I fear no ill,
For Thou art with me, and Thy rod
And staff me comfort still.

My table Thou hast furnished
In the presence of my foes;
My head Thou dost with oil anoint,
And my cup overflows.

Goodness and mercy all my life
Shall surely follow me;
And in God's house forevermore
My dwelling place shall be.

— From the *Scottish Psalter*, 1650

As a youngster I realized that, for my mother
and father, these words were more than poetry.
They were reality. In the last years of my father's

life, he withdrew into himself. I had no idea what he thought about his surroundings in a retirement home or about those who came to visit. I discovered, however, that if I would ask him about the Presbyterian hymnbook and the Twenty-third Psalm as he had sung it as a boy, he would begin to recite those words again. They were like jewels locked in the vault of his mind. Even though he lived behind a mental wall, the Twenty-third Psalm was still precious to him. Like thousands of others, he found that these were words to live by, and also words to die by.

David begins the psalm with a staggering assertion: if the Lord is your Shepherd, you will not want. Those who are in His flock and who trust the Shepherd will not lack for rest because He makes them "to lie down in green pastures." In addition, His sheep will not want for refreshment because He leads His flock "beside still waters."

The word for "still waters" may also be translated "stilled waters." Throughout the psalm David is reflecting on what took place in the shepherd life in Israel. And David knew that sheep have a deathly fear of moving water. Even after a long day in stifling heat, when the sheep come to a rushing stream, they will not drink the cool, clear water. They will stand beside the stream and look, but they will not drink. Fear keeps them from refreshment. They know instinctively that if they should fall into the water, their coats will become water-logged and they will drown. But the shepherd pries loose a few large stones and dams up a quiet place where his sheep may drink. Beside a rushing stream he provides refreshment for the flock with the water he has stilled.

Has your Shepherd ever done this for you? Has it ever seemed to you that some circum-stances of life were more threatening than you could handle? Have you ever drawn back in fear when it seemed that life, like a rampaging river, would suck you under and drown you beneath its flow? Often at such times Christians mutter that "all things work together for good to them that love God, to them who are the called according to his purpose." But even as we repeat those words of Romans 8:28, we are afraid. Then the Shepherd comes and works in those events that we feared most and makes them a place of spiritual refreshment.

Of course, our Shepherd not only leads us to the waters that He has stilled, but if our imagery is correct, He also leads us beside the rushing stream. Do you think that He would lead His flock to a place like that if He did not also plan to provide for their protection and their every need?

Thousands of God's people have joined David in his song. They have found that David's experience is their own. Martha Snell Nicholson, never strong as a child, suffered a complete physical breakdown in early womanhood. She was confined to her bed for more than seven years—years of pain and weakness that almost crushed her strong spirit. Then she went through a series of difficult operations that did little to relieve her pain. Through all this experience she wrote poems that witnessed to her Shepherd's provision in the sickroom. One day Mrs. Nicholson's physician told her that her case was too far advanced to respond to any further treatment. In that hour she expressed her confidence in her Shepherd in a poem titled, "When He Puts Forth His Own Sheep, He Goes Before Them."

*I could not walk this darkening path of pain
    alone;
The years have taken toll of me;
Sometimes my banners droop; my arms have
    grown too tired,
And laughter comes less easily.
And often these—my shrinking cowardly
    eyes—refuse
To face the thing ahead of me.
The certainty of growing pain and helpless-
    ness . . .*

But oh, my Lord is good, for He
Comes quickly to me as I lie there in the dust
Of my defeat and shame and fear;
He stoops and raises me and sets me on my
    feet,
And softly whispers in my ear
That He will never leave me—nay, that He
    will go
Before me all the way. And so
My hand in His, along this brightening path
    of pain,
My Lord and I go together.

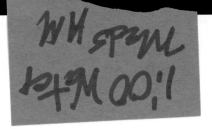

chapter five Close to His Heart

"He restores my soul"

*A*n old nursery rhyme tells the sad tale of Little Bo-Peep who lost her sheep. Someone advised her to "leave them alone, and they'll come home, dragging their tails behind them." We learn at least two things from that little rhyme: first, Bo-Peep wasn't much of a shepherdess; and second, the one to whom she turned for advice didn't know much about sheep. If you ignore sheep that have wandered off, they will seldom wander back.

If you take your dog to the other side of town and try to lose him, he may be back in your front yard before you are. And cats have been known to travel several hundred miles to get back home. But sheep have no sense of direction. When they are lost, they stay lost—until Little Bo-Peep or a shepherd goes to find them.

It is not unusual for sheep to wander away from the flock. A sheep may become interested in a clump of grass, and then another and another, until finally it looks up to discover that it has strayed away from the shepherd and the other sheep. When night comes, a lost sheep is in great danger. Predators lurk in the darkness, eager to pounce and rip the sheep apart. Or, unable to see its way, the sheep may stumble over the side of a cliff or be caught in a thicket.

In the evening when the shepherd returns to the fold, he counts his sheep, calling each by name. If he discovers that one of his flock is still out in the countryside, he leaves his other sheep safely in the fold and trudges back over the route he and the flock covered during the day. He holds a small lantern down close to his feet as he retraces his steps. Calling out in the night, he listens for the bleating of the animal in the darkness. When he finds the sheep, he places it upon his shoulders and carries it back to the fold.

The shepherd will go after a sheep again and again and restore it to the flock. Occasionally, he will have one sheep that makes a habit of staying out late. Every evening when the shepherd counts the flock, the same sheep is missing. Night after night he goes out to seek the lost animal, and night after night he brings it back to the fold. Sometimes, if this wandering becomes a pattern, the shepherd will break the sheep's leg. He makes a splint for the broken leg, but the sheep is still helpless, so the shepherd carries that sheep close to his heart. Then, as the leg begins to mend, the shepherd sets the sheep down by his side. To the limping animal, the smallest stream looms like a giant river. The tiniest knoll rises like a wall. The sheep must depend completely on the shepherd to carry it across the rough terrain. After the leg has healed, however, the sheep has learned a lesson: it stays close to the shepherd's side.

To break the leg of a poor defenseless sheep seems heartless unless you understand the shepherd's motive. Then, what seems to be cruelty is actually kindness. The shepherd knows far better than the sheep the danger of wandering off. He breaks its leg, not to hurt it, but to restore it.

David witnessed the Shepherd's seeking in his own life. When David was in his middle forties, he had an affair with a young married woman by the name of Bathsheba. Their relationship seemed harmless enough until they discovered that Bathsheba was pregnant. David, always in control, knew what he had to do. He summoned Bathsheba's soldier-husband, Uriah, back home from a battle. He planned to get Uriah into bed with his pretty young wife; then what David had done would be covered up. Uriah, however, would not cooperate. As a result, David had Uriah killed. Then he married Bathsheba, and she bore their baby.

David was convinced the entire matter was resolved. But what was a secret on earth was an open scandal in heaven, and God sent the

prophet Nathan to confront the king. When David recognized that God knew what he had done, he repented, crying out for mercy and begging God to forgive him. (You can read his prayer of confession in Psalm 51.) Yet before David ever sought out God, God had sought out David, his wandering sheep.

In a sense, David walked with a limp for the rest of his life. The baby died, several of his sons rebelled against him, and his family disintegrated. God had forgiven him, but forgiveness didn't necessarily wipe out the consequences of David's sin.

God the Shepherd restores His sheep when they wander. When we stray, He seeks us out and brings us back to Himself. He doesn't always deal with us according to our sin or reward us according to our iniquity, but He will do whatever it takes to restore us. In the letter to the Hebrews we find this admonition: "Do not despise the chastening of the Lord, nor be discouraged when you are rebuked by Him;

for whom the LORD loves, He chastens" (12:5–6 NKJV). David experienced God's chastening, and if you are one of God's flock, you will experience it too. It is the mark of the Shepherd's love and concern for you.

chapter six **Following the Shepherd**

*"He guides me in paths
of righteousness"*

*M*any authors have pictured human beings as weary travelers journeying across the wilderness called life. A variety of paths lie before us, and for the most part, we wander on, bewildered, following the first path that attracts us. When we discover that it ends in rocks and thickets, we back off and try another one. We often lament, "If only I knew what to do!" Like sheep, we go astray, wandering our own unguided way.

Yet throughout the centuries millions have testified that in the middle of such uncertainty, they have received guidance from God. David tells us that his Shepherd "leads [us] in the paths of righteousness for His name's sake" (NKJV). Actually, the Hebrew states, "He leads me in the right paths." On many occasions

David must have wondered what to do next. As a farmer, a soldier, and a politician, he lived with the complexity of life and the bewilderment common to all of us. Yet he declares, "I shall not want for guidance."

In the Near East many paths are etched into the terrain. Some have been worn into the landscape by the feet of many travelers; others have been created by winds blowing across the land; and some have been carved out by robbers who want to lead the unsuspecting traveler or shepherd astray and steal his goods or his flock. To the untrained eye these latter two look like real paths; but if you follow them, they lead nowhere or into danger.

David testifies, "He leads me in the right paths." When God guides us, it is not simply to the right places, but to the right kind of life. When it comes to making decisions, we often want to know whether we should take the job in Dallas or move to Chicago; if we should spend our lives in Africa or Latin America. But

God's leading is not primarily to location or vocation. Rather, He leads us to a right life and a mature, godly character.

Years ago I was faced with five different opportunities, all at the same time. At first I was bewildered at the choices. God seemed to be saying, "Before you lie five paths—I dare you to find the right one." But I believed that God was perfectly able to guide me in the choices I had to make. He did, and what I learned was that God's will was not primarily focused on the place He wanted me to be or the job He wanted me to take.

I do not know of any passage in the Bible that tells us whether we should attend college next year or take a new position or get married or go to California. But the Bible clearly reveals God's plan for us. Would you like to know God's will for your life today? The Scriptures tell you. For example, His will for you is, "in every thing give thanks" (1 Thessalonians 5:18). And God's will for you is your "sanctification." That's a large word; but it simply means that we are *set apart* for His purposes (1 Thessalonians 4:3). God's guidance has to do with *what* we are, not *where* we are. If we are *what* God wants us to be, He will have no trouble placing us where He wants us to be. We do not have to be plagued by decisions if we stay close to the Shepherd. He leads us in the right paths and they are paths of righteousness.

Sometimes we feel that God must have lost our address. But the Shepherd knows His sheep by name; He knows who we are and He knows our potential. He will see to it that when we hear His voice and follow Him, He will put us where we ought to be.

Notice that David says, "He leads me" (NKJV). God's direction grows out of a personal relationship. He does not give us a roadmap and tell us to follow it. Instead, He goes before us and leads us to the place of His choosing.

A shepherd in Israel had an interesting way to get the sheep to follow him. As he strolled through a field, he reached up with his staff to a limb of a tree and pulled down a piece of succulent fruit. Then he held the fruit in his hand as he walked before the flock. The sheep, eager to get the tasty tidbit, would crowd close behind the shepherd and nibble at the fruit. The shepherd led them as he fed them, and he fed them as he led them.

One of the ways God leads us is by feeding us through His Word. As we read and study the Scriptures, the Holy Spirit opens its truths to us and shows us the way we ought to go. God's guidance comes to those who hear Him speak and follow what He says.

Notice the assertion: "He leads me . . . for His name's sake" (NKJV). A shepherd values his reputation. If a shepherd were to take a flock into the wilderness and lose that flock, he would be disgraced. You can trust God, the Good Shepherd, not to lead you astray. God is very jealous for His name. All the sheep who follow Him, He guides safely home.

chapter seven **Deep Darkness**

*"Though I walk through the valley
of the shadow of death"*

Chat with the passenger seated next to you on a plane, talk with your hairdresser, or visit with your next-door neighbor and you'll realize that many people are afraid. They are fearful about tomorrow. They don't know what lies over the hill or down the road. Terrible things happen in our world, and they are afraid. Yet we do not have to live in fear. In verse 4 of Psalm 23, David cries, "Yea, though I walk through the valley of the shadow of death, I will fear no evil; for thou art with me." If the Lord is your Shepherd and you are His sheep, you will not want for courage, even when you go through life's most dangerous places.

When we think of a valley, we may imagine a pleasant lowland sweep bounded by sloping

hillsides. But the valley that the psalmist had in mind was a chasm among the hills—a deep, abrupt, faintly lighted ravine with steep, jagged sides and a narrow floor. The phrase "valley of the shadow of death" should be translated "the valley of deep darkness." It was a dreadful, dangerous place for sheep.

Yet the valley, with all its dangers, is part of the shepherd's plan. Notice how this verse relates to the one that precedes it. In verse 3, David declares, "He leads me in the paths of righteousness for His name's sake" (NKJV). Verse 4 goes on to say that one of the paths through which the shepherd takes the flock is the valley of deep darkness.

In springtime the flocks graze in the lowlands. Then, as summer comes, the snows in the mountains melt and the shepherd leads his flock up to better grazing land. To take the flock to better pastures, however, he must lead them through some treacherous and threatening ravines. Hidden in the shadows along this

dark pathway are serpents, coiled to strike; and wolves, ready to pounce upon the sheep to destroy them. Yet the sheep can go through this dark ravine with courage because they know their shepherd has led them there.

Undoubtedly, as David wrote this psalm, he could remember how as a boy he had led his own flocks through the valley of deep darkness. He could hear the distant howl of a wolf or the cry of a hyena lying in wait for his flock. David remembered how his sheep huddled close to his heels, and how he was prepared to fight for their lives. Perhaps the elderly king had scars on his arms or his feet that he had received while fending off enemies of his flock. David knew that the life of a man or woman also has dangerous passages. But just as the sheep trusted David for protection, so he had learned to trust God to protect him. David knew that when he came to the deep shaded valleys of life, he did not have to be afraid, because the Shepherd was with him and would protect him.

What kind of courage does a sheep need? A sheep does not need courage to fight its enemies. The most courageous sheep in the world would be an easy victim of the smallest wolf or mountain lion. What a sheep needs is courage to trust the shepherd. When it senses that a predator is near, it looks up to see the shepherd nearby, and then it goes back to grazing again. That takes courage!

What kind of courage does a Christian need? We don't need courage to fight our own spiritual battles. We have an enemy not made of blood and flesh, an enemy we cannot see or touch. He is an enemy who would destroy us, if he could. What kind of courage does a Christian need? We need courage to trust the Shepherd. If we know that He is nearby, we simply trust ourselves to Him and go back to grazing again. And that takes courage!

What threatening shadows lie across your path today? What dangers do you face? Your Shepherd knows them all, and if you trust

yourself to Him, you can have courage. Listen to this good word from God: "Do not be anxious about anything, but in everything, by prayer and petition, with thanksgiving, present your requests to God. And the peace of God, which transcends all understanding, will guard your hearts and your minds in Christ Jesus" (Philippians 4:6–7 NIV).

chapter eight **The Darkest Valley**

"I will fear no evil"

*P*robably the most familiar sentence in Psalm 23 is, "Yea, though I walk through the valley of the shadow of death, I will fear no evil, for thou art with me." When David wrote those words, he may not have been thinking of death at all. He was saying that he had the courage to go through life's most fearful experiences because he had a Shepherd who had led him there, a Shepherd who would shield him from danger.

It is not without significance, though, that the sentence has been translated for centuries as "the valley of the shadow of death." Death is the darkest valley that lies before us. We fear for our loved ones who go through it, and we are afraid when we face it ourselves. Of all our enemies, death is not only the last, it is the worst. And we reveal our fear by not facing up to death. We cover it with flowers or talk about it in euphemisms. Yet David knew the dark place of death, and he faced it with courage.

Notice the intriguing change of pronouns in the middle of Psalm 23. In the first three verses David has been talking *about* the Shepherd, but then in verse 4 he talks *to* the Shepherd. "Yea, though I walk through the valley of the shadow of death, I will fear no evil for *thou* art with me" (emphasis added). The psalmist has turned from praise to prayer.

Perhaps David remembered the times when Saul, insane with jealousy, pursued him into the wilderness and into the mountains to try to kill him. Perhaps he thought of enemies who would, even as he wrote, have slain him to rob him of his throne. And when he felt the clammy hand of fear squeezing his heart, he wrote, "I will not be afraid, for you are with me."

A mother and her small son traveled from Chicago to California by train. As small boys do, the lad got restless. He got up from his seat, went to the end of the car, and got a drink of water. He came back to his seat, and a few moments later ran down to the end of the car again. After this happened several times, a woman sitting across the aisle felt sorry for the mother. She called the youngster over and said, "That's a lovely sailor suit you have on." The boy explained, "My mommy made it. She sewed on these buttons and put the stripes on my sleeves. And she even put a buckle on my pants." As he was telling the woman what his mother had done, the train plunged into a tunnel and the car was blanketed in darkness. The little boy left the woman and scooted across the aisle; he threw his arms around his mother's legs and said, "Mommy, Mommy, you're here and I'm not scared, am I?"

It was one thing to talk about his mother while the train was in the sunshine. But in the darkness he no longer talked about his mother; he talked to her. David was doing something like that. As long as he thought about rest and refreshment and lush green pastures, he talked about the Shepherd. But when he thought about the dark valleys in life, through which he had passed, and the darkest valley through which he was sure to go, he spoke to God directly. "When I go through those places, you are with me."

Sorrow and death can make the presence of the Shepherd very real. He knows the way to death and through death. After all, He traveled through the valley of death Himself, and He came out victorious on the other side. Because He is with us, we can be certain that He can do the same for us.

In the last book of the Bible, the risen Christ, our Shepherd, tells us, "Do not be afraid; I am the First and the Last. I am He who lives, and was dead, and behold, I am alive forevermore. Amen. And I have the keys of Hades and of Death" (Revelation 1:17–18 NKJV). The Lord Jesus Christ wants you to trust Him; and through His presence He can empower you to live triumphantly and to face death with courage.

chapter nine His Powerful Love

*"Your rod and your staff,
they comfort me"*

*T*he Scriptures refer to sheep, lambs, ewes, sheepfolds, and shepherds about six hundred times. God seems to say, *If you want to learn something about Christians, watch sheep; and if you want to know something about me, watch a faithful shepherd.* As we have seen, Israel's greatest king, David, described his relationship with God as that of a sheep to the Shepherd. In verse 4 of Psalm 23, David declares that because he is God's sheep and God is his shepherd, he will not lack for comfort. "Thy rod and thy staff they comfort me."

The rod and the staff symbolize God's power. The rod—a wooden club about two feet long—was used to defend the flock against attacking animals. It had a round head, usually whittled from the knot of a tree bough, into which the shepherd pounded sharp bits of stone or metal. A skilled shepherd not only wielded the club to smash the head of the attacker, but he could also hurl the club like a missile to strike a predator lurking in the distance.

The shepherd's staff, or crook, was bent at one end. With his staff, the shepherd restrained the sheep from wandering, or hooked their legs to pull them out of holes into which they had stumbled. He also used it to pull back branches when a sheep became tangled in a thicket, or to beat back high grass to drive out serpents coiled in the path.

The sheep takes comfort from the shepherd's power. "Your rod and your staff they comfort me." The word *comfort* means "with strength." But we have diluted the concept of comfort so that it has become merely a nice-sounding phrase. We say, "Cheer up! Things will get better" to comfort someone. Yet deep inside we suspect that things may get worse.

We have nothing but words to smooth and quiet and calm.

God offers His people more than a hand-kerchief to dry their tears. He offers them His power and His might. But frankly, we tend to be a bit afraid of God's power, so that the thought of His power by itself doesn't provide much comfort. When we look up into the night sky and see a million stars, or consider the universe that God has made, we are in awe, but we don't necessarily feel comforted. We may even be unsettled by His power. In fact, we may think of God as the ancients thought of the mythic gods on Mount Olympus. We may suspect that He will hurl cancer into our lives simply to show us He is boss.

But David's Shepherd and our Shepherd is as tender as He is powerful. God is the most self-obligated Being in the universe. He cannot use His power outside His love, just as He can-not exercise His holiness apart from His grace. God's might is at the service of His heart. The enemies of the Shepherd may fear the rod and the staff, but the sheep receive comfort from them. They know these weapons will be used only in their defense.

When our daughter Vicki was about three years old, she became very ill. The doctor came to our home, and as soon as he saw her, he rushed her to the hospital. As we entered the emergency room, he took me aside and told me to prepare myself because he wasn't sure that she would live through the night. I stood in a dimly lit hospital room and watched helplessly as our daughter struggled for her life. I gladly would have climbed into her crib and fought her battle for her, but I was helpless. Sometime in the middle of the night, I took some comfort in knowing that God loved us and that He loved our child. After all, He gave Himself to die for us. I knew, therefore, that He desired only our highest good. I loved Vicki dearly, yet I was helpless to do what my love desired. Then it occurred to me that God who loved us was also a God of unlimited power. He had the power to do what His love dictated.

If God chose to take Vicki from us, this would be a loving choice. If she went to be with Him, then it would be the best thing for her and for us. My love was limited, but God's love was not. And in that dark hour I experienced the comfort of God.

How much comfort would it give us if our "whys" were answered? Why the child had to contract that deadly virus? Why the road was icy just then? Why was the loved one on that fatal flight? If God merely gave us answers— scientific or philosophical explanations for our bruising questions—how much comfort would that give us? A child isn't comforted by being told why his toy broke or why her finger was bruised in the car door or why he must be given the shot. The child is comforted by knowing that his mother loves him and believing she can do something about his hurt.

From the rod and staff of the Shepherd we derive comfort, not only for ourselves but for others. You can comfort others when you are able to share with them the comfort that God has given you. Paul, the early church leader, wrote, "Blessed be God, even the Father of our Lord Jesus Christ, the Father of mercies, and the God of all comfort; who comforteth us in all our tribulation, that we may be able to comfort them which are in any trouble, by the comfort wherewith we ourselves are comforted of God" (2 Corinthians 1:3–4).

chapter ten **Protecting the Sheep**

"You anoint my head with oil"

*I*t has always been dangerous to be alive. Not only are we threatened with crashes and sickness and lightning bolts, but we live in territory that has never been a friend to God or to His people. Three thousand years ago David had a bracing word for those—which means all of us—who live in dangerous times: "Thou preparest a table before me in the presence of mine enemies; thou anointest my head with oil" (Psalm 23:5).

Some commentators believe that the Twenty-third Psalm changes images between verses 4 and 5. The first four verses, they say, describe David's relationship to God in terms of a sheep with its shepherd, whereas verses 5 and 6 picture the relationship as a banquet prepared by a host for a friend. They may be right.

But I agree with Charles W. Slemming who has studied shepherds of the Middle East; and who insists that this verse, too, pictures shepherd life in Israel. When a shepherd enters a new field where he can feed his flock, he walks up and down inspecting the ground closely, looking for grass that might poison the sheep. He also searches the field for vipers. These tiny brown adders live under the ground, and they pop out of their small holes and nip the noses of the sheep. Their bite is poisonous, and the inflammation can kill the animal.

The shepherd protects the sheep in two ways. When he finds the vipers' holes, he takes a bottle of thick oil from his girdle; then, raking over any long grass with his staff, he pours a circle of oil at the top of every viper's hole he can find. Secondly, as he leads the sheep into the field, he anoints the head of each animal with the oil. When the vipers attempt to crawl out of their holes to bite the sheep, the oil keeps them from getting out. The smooth bodies of the vipers cannot pass over the slippery oil, and they are kept as prisoners inside their holes. The oil on the sheep's head also acts as a repellent. If a viper should get near a sheep, the smell of the oil drives the viper away. Literally, therefore, the sheep graze in the presence of their enemies.

God sends His people to live in dangerous places. Jesus told His disciples, "I send you forth as sheep in the midst of wolves" (Matthew 10:16). The most dangerous place for a sheep to be is in the midst of a wolf pack.

For many Christians, life with God consists of attending worship services, going to religious seminars, or having Christian friends over for coffee and cake. Although such people can seem quite religious, they are disobedient. Jesus sent us into our society to live for Him there. "I do not pray that You should take them out of the world," He prayed to the Father, "but that You should keep them from the evil one. They are not of the world just as I am not of the world. Sanctify them by Your truth. Your word is truth" (John 17:15–17 NKJV). Jesus did not pray that His followers would be removed from the world. He prayed only that they would be protected from the Evil One who governs the world.

How did Jesus relate to His own society? The religious leaders of His day attacked Jesus because He associated with disreputable people. He ate with pimps and prostitutes, pickpockets and hustlers. He cultivated their friendship, and they enjoyed spending time with Him. As Jesus related to the world, we are to relate to the world. We are to be the light of the world, of society, but light is useless unless it penetrates the darkness.

One reason we fail to cultivate the friendship of unbelievers is that we consider the prospect to be dangerous. We do not invite them to our homes for dinner or associate with them socially because we feel that their values could easily become our values. Admittedly, that is a possibility if we are not trusting our Shepherd. We *are* to be separate from the world, in that we are to be distinct by the way we live; but we not to be isolated from those who do not know God.

One way we become distinct is through Bible study. Jesus prayed, "Sanctify them by Your truth" (NKJV). The word *sanctify* means "set apart." So, in essence, our Lord prayed, "Set them apart through their study of Your Word." As we study the Scriptures and appropriate what we learn about God to our lives, we can graze safely in dangerous pastures. What the ancient shepherd did for his sheep, God does for us.

In His final words to His followers before He returned to heaven, Jesus commanded, "Go therefore and make disciples of all the nations" (Matthew 28:18–20 NKJV). Have you ever wondered what the word *therefore* is there for? In introducing this commission, Jesus asserted that "all authority has been given to

Me in heaven and on earth." At the close of the commission, He declared, "I am with you always." He sends us into the world, backed by His authority and protected by His presence. Of course, it is dangerous to live in enemy territory, but God directs us to dangerous places and it is there that He prepares a table for us. We are far safer in such a place with God than we could possibly be anywhere else without Him.

chapter eleven **The Abundance of Faith**

"My cup overflows"

*W*e all know people who have developed griping into a fine art. They can look at any situation and tell you what is wrong with it. Unfortunately, a few of these sour spirits have gotten into our churches.

When you listen to these disgruntled people, you know they are poverty-stricken. That does not mean they do not have money. They often do. But although they may have fat purses, they have thin souls. Christians who sing the song of heaven in a minor key don't impress others with the richness of their faith. We are attracted to the reality of Jesus Christ by those who exclaim with the psalmist, "My cup runs over"!

That may sound easy enough for David to say. After all, he reigned as a powerful king, with servants to do his bidding. But David

knew hard times. Two of his sons, Absalom and Adonijah, turned against him and tried to steal his throne. One of David's trusted advisors betrayed him, and his army chief deserted him. At one point in his life, David lived as Public Enemy #1 for ten years. And that's just a partial list of his trials and tribulations. Yet in spite of all of that, David insisted that he drank from an overflowing cup.

David wasn't talking about someone spilling water in his lap. He was thinking about how a considerate shepherd provided for his sheep. Shepherds often drew water for their flocks from very deep wells. Many of these cisterns were a hundred feet or more in depth. To draw the water, a shepherd used a leather bucket at the end of a long rope. The bucket held about three quarts, and the shepherd had to let it down and draw it up hand-over-hand. Then he poured the water into large stone cups beside the well. It was a long and tiring process. If a shepherd had fifty sheep, he might have to draw water for two hours or more to allow the sheep to drink all they wanted. Sheep do not like to get wet. So it was a mark of a shepherd's special kindness to keep the stone cups filled to the brim so each sheep could drink with ease.

A hireling shepherd would not demonstrate the same care for the flock. As soon as the sheep had half enough water, the hireling would shove it aside so he would not have to draw more. But David's Shepherd had no such disposition. He drew and drew and filled the cups to overflowing. He was untiring in His efforts to satisfy the thirsty flock.

God is a great giver! He lavishes His bounties on us. He gives us not only what we ask or think; He gives us abundantly above what we ask or think. He not only gives us abundantly above what we ask or think; He gives us *exceedingly abundantly* above all that we ask or think.

It's astonishing how we can take God's bounty for granted. Have you ever had a time

in your life when you were not sure where
your next meal was coming from? Then, at the
last moment, God provided a bowl of soup and
a hunk of bread and you were very thankful
for His supply. Yet when He gives us so much
food that we have to count calories to keep
from eating too much, we sit down at the table
with little more than a casual word of thanks,
and then we complain about how difficult the
day was. When we do not reflect on His goodness, our souls get thin.

God not only provides an abundance of
goods for us, He is also abundant in His forgiveness. That is the glad message of the
Bible. As Christians we are forgiven fully,
freely, finally, forever. But we can easily take
His pardon for granted. As H. G. Wells once
remarked, "Forgiveness? Of course, God for-
gives—that's His business."

Dwight L. Moody was a famous evangelist in the nineteenth century. On Thanksgiving Day, 1899, he spoke at the penitentiary at

Canon City, Colorado. When the governor learned that Moody would be at the prison, he wrote to him and enclosed a pardon for a woman who had served three years of a ten-year sentence. After speaking to the inmates, Mr. Moody produced the pardon, saying, "I have a pardon in my hands for one of the prisoners seated here today." He had intended to say something more, but he saw that the strain caused by his announcement was so severe that he dared not leave the prisoners in suspense. Calling the woman's name, he invited her to come forward to accept the governor's Thanksgiving gift.

The woman hesitated for a moment, then got up, uttered a shriek, and fell sobbing and laughing across the lap of the woman seated next to her. Her excitement was so intense that Moody could do nothing more than to make a brief application to illustrate God's offer of pardon and peace. Afterward, the evangelist observed that if Christians showed such excite-

ment after accepting the pardon offered by Jesus Christ, people would label them fanatics.

The old hymn invites us to count our blessings and name them one by one. If you do that, you'll discover that, like David, you too drink from an overflowing cup.

chapter twelve **Hope for the Future**

*"Surely goodness and mercy will follow me
all the days of my life"*

*S*ome people look for trouble. They worry about all the horrible things that could happen tomorrow. But David looked to the future with confidence. He asserts at the end of Psalm 23, "Surely goodness and mercy shall follow me all the days of my life." David had lived a full life. He had endured the rage of battle and heard the acclaim of the nation. He had climbed to the heights and had fallen to the depths. Few of us crowd so much into life. And David looked to the future with happy anticipation.

In this final sentence, the psalmist moves from his past experiences to his present and future life with God. His past experiences gave birth to his present hope. Because David had seen God's faithfulness through the years, he had hope for the years to come.

God sends goodness and mercy to follow us. Goodness is getting those things we do not deserve. The goodness of God is found in abundance and invades every area of our lives. You can live life with confidence if you recognize the goodness of God. Of course, there will be harsh experiences that you will not be able to explain. But you can get through them when you realize that a good God orders your days.

A good God cannot fulfill every wish. We do not give a child poison to play with, no matter how much he begs for it—not if we're good parents. We don't keep our children home from school merely because they do not want to go. A good parent does what is best for a daughter or son, even when the youngster cannot understand.

David does not say that all kinds of good things will come into his life to make him a spoiled brat. The goodness of God is not goodness as a child may view it. Instead, it is God's goodness that brings us through the events of our lives so that we will be molded into mature men and women.

Paul declares in Romans, "All things work together for good to those who love God, to those who are the called according to His purpose" (8:28 NKJV). Does that mean that cancer is good and we should be happy about it? Of course not. Does it mean that death is good? No, death is an enemy. It means that God works through all things so that together they mold us into the people He wants us to be. A cook puts a great many different ingredients into a cake. Not all of the ingredients taste good in and of themselves. Yet, in the hand of a competent homemaker, the bitter and sweet are blended together to become a delicious cake. Thus the Good Shepherd orders the events of our lives so that ultimately we will become what He wants us to be.

The psalmist was also sure that mercy would follow him. The Hebrew word is *hesed*, which is sometimes translated "lovingkindness"

or "loyal love." The New Testament would render it as "grace." *Hesed* is grace given to men and women who do not deserve it.

The judge of all the earth has a cause against us because of our sin. If He doles out justice, we will be separated from Him forever. Any one of our sins would shut us off from God, just as darkness is destroyed in the presence of light. But God is gracious and merciful. Through the death of Jesus Christ, who paid the penalty we should have paid for our sins, God acts in loyal love. The death of Jesus Christ allows Him to provide both forgiveness and cleansing. We do not have to fear the future because we know that nothing—absolutely nothing—neither our circumstances nor our sin, can separate us from our Shepherd, Jesus Christ. He who has been faithful in the past will continue to be faithful until the end.

Surely goodness and mercy will pursue us. "Surely," because God has never failed us in the past. "Surely," because He does not begin a work He does not complete. "Surely," because the experience of His flock attests to what David knew: that God never forsakes us. If the Lord is your Shepherd and you are His sheep, He walks before you, and goodness and mercy will follow you all the days of your life. That includes today.

chapter thirteen **In His Presence**

"I will dwell in the house
of the LORD forever"

*I*f someone were to ask you, "What is a Christian?" what would you say?

Christians attend church. They should live distinctive lives. They believe certain important facts about God. But essentially, being a Christian is not about any of those things. Christianity is a relationship with the most wonderful person in the universe, Jesus, the Christ.

In Psalm 23, David talks about the personal relationship he enjoyed with God. He declares that if the Lord is your Shepherd and you are His sheep, you will not lack for anything that you need at any time. Looking back on his life, David tells us that his Shepherd has provided rest and refreshment, restoration and guidance, courage and comfort, protection and security.

And what is more, David looks to the future with a sturdy confidence.

The Shepherd does many things for us. But you will have missed the meaning of the psalm unless you realize that David is singing about his personal, intimate relationship with God Himself. David ends the Twenty-third Psalm with the affirmation, "I will dwell in the house of the LORD forever." Although many readers think of heaven when they read these words, David did not have heaven in mind. He was not thinking precisely *where* he would be in the future, but *with whom* he would be.

In Psalm 27, David says, "One thing I have desired of the LORD, that will I seek; that I may dwell in the house of the LORD all the days of my life, to behold the beauty of the LORD, and to inquire in His temple" (Psalm 27:4 NKJV). David wanted to be in the temple, the Lord's house, because there he would be in the Lord's presence. Whatever else heaven may be, it is primarily a place where we will be *with Christ*.

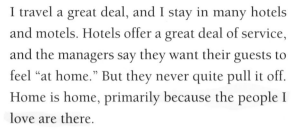

I travel a great deal, and I stay in many hotels and motels. Hotels offer a great deal of service, and the managers say they want their guests to feel "at home." But they never quite pull it off. Home is home, primarily because the people I love are there.

Just before Jesus left the earth, He told His followers, "Let not your heart be troubled. . . . I go to prepare a place for you. . . . I will come again, and receive you to Myself; that where I am, you may be also" (John 14:1–3 NASB). These words brushed away their tears because they had His promise that they would be with Him. We who are Christ's sheep can be sure that our Shepherd, who has led us safely through life, will see us safely to His home to live with Him.

G. Campbell Morgan was a noted pastor who served churches both in England and the United States. Early in his ministry, a young woman from his church lay dying. She had given birth to a baby, and it seemed likely that it would cost her her life. Dr. Morgan went to visit the young mother and stood in the shadows of the room while her doctor did his best to take care of her. She was delirious and kept saying, "I don't want to go alone. Please. Please. I want to take my baby with me."

The physician tried to say something that would help her. "Your baby will have loving care. You need not be afraid. You can't take the baby with you. The gate through which you may go is wide enough for only one." Campbell Morgan stepped forward and touched the physician's shoulder and said, "Doctor, don't tell her that. Tell her that the gate through which she is about to pass is wide enough for two—for herself and her Savior. He has brought her to this place and will not desert her now. He will see her safely home to the other side."

If at the end of our journey, death wins, then what's the use? But we live in certainty that when we come to the end of life, the Shep-

herd will not throw us into some ditch of a grave and forget us. He will be there to take us to be with Him.

Psalm 23 begins and ends with the Lord. "The Lord is my shepherd. . . . I will dwell in the house of the Lord forever." Christianity begins and ends with the Lord Jesus Christ. You become a Christian by committing all that you are to all that you know of Christ. And you grow as a Christian by knowing more of Him. Do you know Him? I'm not asking whether you know *about* Him. Thousands of men and women brought up in Sunday school and church know all the facts, but they don't know Him. I don't mean, "Do you know the Twenty-third Psalm?" Hundreds of people who may not know the Shepherd recite the psalm. But do you know *Him?*

Jesus calls you to Himself. "Come to Me, all you who labor and are heavy laden, and I will give you rest" (Matthew 11:28 NKJV). "Whoever believes in Him should not perish but have eternal life" (John 3:16 NKJV). "As many as received Him, to them He gave the right to become children of God" (John 1:12 NKJV).

You can know that the Lord is a shepherd, but that will not do you much good. You can even understand that the Lord is *the* Shepherd—the only Person in the universe who can fully meet your deepest needs. It is only when you place your confidence in Him personally, however, that you can sing with David, "The LORD is *my* Shepherd; I shall not want." And it is then that you can affirm with conviction, based on God's promise, "I will dwell in the house of the LORD forever."

If the Lord is indeed your Shepherd, you will not lack for anything you really need . . . forever.

Note to Reader

*T*he publisher invites you to share your response to the message of this book by writing Discovery House Publishers, Box 3566, Grand Rapids, MI 49501, USA. For information about other Discovery House books, music, or videos, contact us at the same address or call 1-800-653-8333. Find us on the Internet at http://www.dhp.org/ or send e-mail to books@dhp.org.